- 2

Dealing with Drugs

Inhalants and Solvents

Jon Eben Field

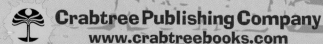

Crabtree Publishing Company
www.crabtreebooks.com

Developed and produced by: Plan B Book Packagers
www.planbbookpackagers.com

Editorial director: Ellen Rodger

Art director: Rosie Gowsell-Pattison

Editor: Molly Aloian

Proofreader: Wendy Scavuzzo

Cover design: Margaret Amy Salter

Project coordinator: Kathy Middleton

**Production coordinator and
  prepress technician:** Katherine Berti

Print coordinator: Katherine Berti

Photographs:
Front cover: © Jennie Hart / Alamy; Title page:
Available Light/iStockphoto.com; p. 6: Luxor
Photo/Shutterstock.com; p. 8: Elena Elisseeva/
Shutterstock.com; p. 9: Dmitrijs Dmitrijevs/
Shutterstock.com; p. 10: F. Lariviere/Shutterstock.com;
p. 11: (middle) Dzarek/Shutterstock.com, (left) Petr
Malyshev/Shutterstock.com, (right) Abramov Timur/
Shutterstock.com; p. 12: Lucian Coman/
Shutterstock.com; p. 15: (left) Magic Vision/
Shutterstock.com, (right) Winiki/Shutterstock.com;
p. 16: Dusko/Shutterstock.com; p. 17: Yellow J./
Shutterstock.com; p. 18: Daniel Alvarez/
Shutterstock.com; p. 19: Lisey Kina/Shutterstock.com;
p. 20: Eky Studio/Shutterstock.com; p. 21: Kamira/
Shutterstock.com; p. 22: Oleksii Natykach/
Shutterstock.com; p. 23: Reflekta/Shutterstock.com;
p. 24: Allyson Kitts/Shutterstock.com; p. 25: Tracing
Tea/Shutterstock.com; p. 26: K. Dimitris/
Shutterstock.com; p. 27: EML/Shutterstock.com;
p. 28-29: Emi Cristea/Shutterstock.com; p. 30: Oto
Art/Shutterstock.com; p. 31: NorGal/
Shutterstock.com; p. 32: Suzanne Tucker/
Shutterstock.com; p. 36: Galina Barskaya/
Shutterstock.com; p. 37: Little NY/Shutterstock.com;
p. 38: Viktor Gladkov/Shutterstock.com; p. p. 41:

Library and Archives Canada Cataloguing in Publication

Field, Jon Eben, 1975-
    Inhalants and solvents / Jon Eben Field.

(Dealing with drugs)
Includes index.
Issued also in electronic formats.
ISBN 978-0-7787-5508-1 (bound).--ISBN 978-0-7787-5515-9 (pbk.)

    1. Inhalant abuse--Juvenile literature. I. Title.
II. Series: Dealing with drugs (St. Catharines, Ont.)

HV5822.S65F53 2011   j362.29'93   C2011-905635-6

Library of Congress Cataloging-in-Publication Data

Field, Jon Eben.
Inhalants and solvents / Jon Eben Field.
    p. cm. -- (Dealing with drugs)
  Includes index.
  ISBN 978-0-7787-5508-1 (reinforced library binding : alk. paper)
-- ISBN 978-0-7787-5515-9 (pbk. : alk. paper) -- ISBN 978-1-4271-
8823-6 (electronic pdf) -- ISBN 978-1-4271-9726-9 (electronic
html)
  1. Inhalant abuse--Juvenile literature. I. Title.

HV5822.S65F54 2012
362.29'93--dc23

2011032621

Crabtree Publishing Company

www.crabtreebooks.com   1-800-387-7650

Printed in the U.S.A./112011/JA20111018

Published in Canada
Crabtree Publishing
616 Welland Ave.
St. Catharines, Ontario
L2M 5V6

Published in the United States
Crabtree Publishing
PMB 59051
350 Fifth Avenue, 59th Floor
New York, New York 10118

Published in the United Kingdom
Crabtree Publishing
Maritime House
Basin Road North, Hove
BN41 1WR

Published in Australia
Crabtree Publishing
3 Charles Street
Coburg North
VIC 3058

Facts & Stats

- The are over 2,000 different household products that can be abused as inhalants or solvents.

- According to a 2008 National Survey on drug use, there were 729,000 individuals 12 years old or older who had used inhalants and solvents for the first time within that year.

- The highest rate of inhalant and solvent abuse is found among grade 8 students.

- Inhalants and solvents have existed throughout much of history, but significant abuse began only in the 20th century.

- Individuals can die from inhalant and solvent abuse through a syndrome called sudden sniffing death.

Introduction
All Huffed Up

Have you ever been pressured by a friend, or tempted by loneliness or stress, to get high by inhaling everyday substances found in your home? **Inhalants** and **solvents** are substances that give off chemical fumes that act like drugs when breathed in. They exist almost everywhere in the home but that doesn't make them safe. The spray paint in your family's closet or garage contain gases that can be inhaled. Whip cream and other **aerosol** cans also contain these gases. Other common solvents such as gasoline, model glue, and nail polish remover are readily available, but they are far from harmless. In fact, inhalants and solvents are as dangerous as street drugs. Users can die from a heart attack with their first use.

Inhalant and solvent use is particularly dangerous because of how the chemicals harm your body and brain. These substances were not created to be inhaled. They are powerful cleaners, **propellants**, and **accelerants**. When inhaled, they enter the bloodstream within seconds and affect how we see, feel, and think. With so many chemical ingredients interacting, medical experts do not yet fully understand all the ways these substances cause harm.

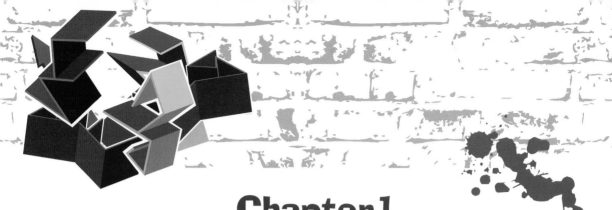

Chapter 1
What's the Big Deal?

Studies show inhalant and solvent abuse is highest among grade 8 students, but the chemicals huffed or sniffed are not child's play. Experimenting with inhalants is risky. Users can die—even from the first time they try it. They can suffocate, **asphyxiate**, choke on their own vomit, or make other thoughtless and reckless decisions that may seem fun when they are under the influence. Inhalants and solvents are highly addictive and cause brain damage and harm vital organs.

Volatile solvents such as gasoline or nail polish remover are the most common inhalants and solvents used by youth to get high. These are liquids that rapidly **evaporate** at room temperature into vapors, or fumes. The vapors from solvents are inhaled into the lungs and users experience a brief, **disorienting** high. The high may make users feel dizzy, euphoric (extremely happy), nauseous, or giddy. The high ordinarily disappears within a few minutes to half an hour and then some users feel depressed and sad. Many begin inhaling vapors again almost immediately to recreate and extend the feeling of being high.

Why Get High?

What causes a person to want to get high in the first place?
One common answer is boredom. Adolescence is a difficult
period of growth and transition. Many youths feel disconnected
from family members and rely on their friends for support.
Boredom can feel bleak or harsh. Inhalants and solvents
are used to ease the boredom—and they are easy to find.
Sometimes, friends encourage experimentation. Peer pressure
often sounds like this: "Hey, everybody's doing it. It's not big
deal." Or "C'mon, it's crazy fun. You'll love it." Or even
"Just try a little bit. It won't hurt, I promise."

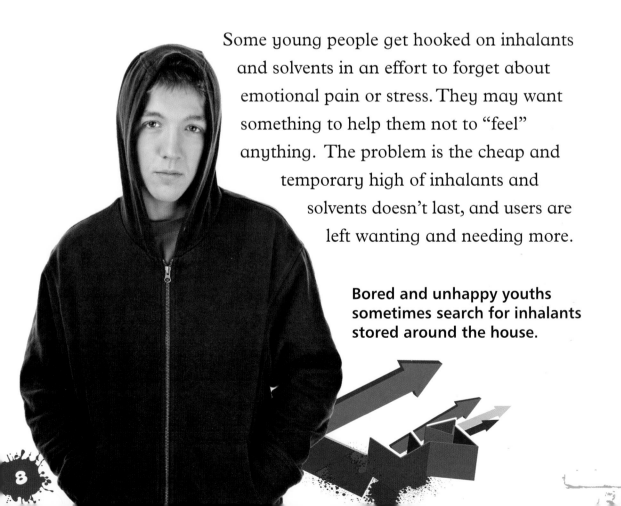

Some young people get hooked on inhalants
and solvents in an effort to forget about
emotional pain or stress. They may want
something to help them not to "feel"
anything. The problem is the cheap and
temporary high of inhalants and
solvents doesn't last, and users are
left wanting and needing more.

**Bored and unhappy youths
sometimes search for inhalants
stored around the house.**

How They Work

Because inhalants and solvents come in so many different forms, they interact with the body in many ways. Once the inhalant or solvent is inhaled into the lungs, it rapidly enters the bloodstream. The chemicals are quickly transported in the blood throughout the body and begin to affect the brain and **nervous system**. The high experienced from inhalants can make people feel "drunk" or confused. The effects of inhalation rapidly disappear, or are lost within minutes, and the user often begins inhaling again. Users can feel dizzy and nauseous. These sensations result from a lack of oxygen in the brain and the concentration of solvents in the blood.

Inhalants and solvents have a **depressive** effect on the body's nervous system. The body slows down its functions. Users feel disembodied, or separate from his or her body. With extreme **intoxication**, the user will pass out.

Inhalant use can cause hallucinations, extreme dizziness, slurred speech, increased heart rate, and distortions of space and time.

Sudden Sniffing Death Syndrome

Studies have shown that 22 percent of inhalant and solvent sniffing deaths occur the first time that someone tries sniffing. That's a frightening statistic! Sudden sniffing death syndrome (SSDS) occurs with alarming frequency in inhalant and solvent abuse and is directly linked to the abuse of propane and butane, the chemical in cigarette lighters. Almost all inhalants have an **anesthetic** effect on the body. This means that when using inhalants, your body and

brain are slowly being put to sleep by the chemicals in the gases and inhaled vapors. Butane and many aerosols make your body highly sensitive to noradrenaline, the chemical your body produces when you're frightened or exerting yourself physically. When intoxicated users are suddenly startled, have a delusion, or are frightened, the rush of noradrenaline can cause irregular heartbeats, leading to a heart attack. With SSDS, inhalant users can die within minutes of inhaling vapors.

Mind Altering

Inhalants and solvents are psychoactive, meaning that they change the way a user thinks or behaves.

Huffing, Bagging, Sniffing, Dusting

On the street, the term "sniffing" describes direct inhalation of the solvent from a canister. "Huffing" is the street lingo used to describe when the solvent or inhalant is poured or sprayed on a cloth, and then inhaled, or "huffed." The terms are so common that many inhalants and solvents are simply known as "huff" or "sniff." "Bagging" happens when a user places a liquid, such as gasoline, or a gas such as nitrous oxide (often from a can of whipped cream) in a bag and then inhales the fumes out of the bag. The term "dusting" describes inhaling the fumes from aerosol cans primarily used to dust or clean electronic equipment. "Dusting" also refers to spraying aerosols directly into the user's mouth.

Bags and cloths are used to inhale fumes.

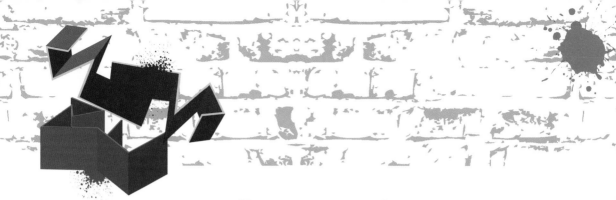

Chapter 2
Store Shelf High

Thousands of common household products are considered dangerous when inhaled. These products, from glues and paints to cleaners, air fresheners, and cooking sprays, were never designed to be deliberately sniffed or inhaled into the lungs. People use them for their intended purposes every day. Almost all of these products are available both legally and cheaply in grocery stores, drugstores, and hardware stores. They are cheap, commonly found, and legal, so many young people choose inhalants as their drug of first-time use.

Gateway to Other Drugs?

Inhalants and solvents are much like other highly addictive drugs in that they may get the user high for a short period of time, but the trade-off is a growing need for more. Huffers often think that their habit is not harmful and easy to quit, but the reality is that inhalant abuse is deadly and hard to kick. Inhalants and solvents are considered "gateway drugs" because many users graduate to using other drugs—ones that give them a longer or more intense high—when huffing no longer works.

What's in Them?

Inhalants and solvents are divided into four main categories. Each of them includes psychoactive agents, meaning that they affect how our brain works. Volatile solvents are the most commonly abused forms of inhalants and solvents. Solvents are liquids that dissolve other substances. They are volatile, or subject to change, because they begin to rapidly evaporate when exposed to the air. Volatile solvents are chemicals such as toluene (model glue) and acetone (nail polish remover). Other products, such as gasoline, paint thinners, White Out, and felt-tip markers, contain a number of solvents and other chemicals. These solvents are often sniffed straight from an open container or huffed from a cloth.

Pressurized Liquids

Some inhalants and solvents come as pressurized liquids or gases in aerosol cans. These include hydrofluorocarbon gases (refrigerants), aerosols, and other propellants. These pressurized liquids and gases, used in spray paint cans, and hair spray, propel the substances from the can into the air. Some users spray aerosol cans into a cloth and then inhale. Other aerosols are used in "dusting"—or when the user sprays the gas directly into his or her mouth.

Poor Man's Pot

Inhalants are frequently referred to as "poor man's pot" because they are relatively cheap—making them a drug of choice for young people and those who cannot afford other expensive drugs.

Gases

Gases such as nitrous oxide (laughing gas), propane, and butane make up another category of inhalants. Nitrous oxide is an anesthetic gas used by dentists. Inhaling nitrous oxide makes people feel lightheaded and causes them to giggle and laugh. This is why it is called laughing gas. Butane is a flammable gas made from petroleum and is used as a fuel in lighters. When inhaled, butane causes sleepiness. It also causes the larynx to spasm, preventing users from breathing for up to several minutes. Unable to breathe, but deeply sedated, some butane abusers die from lack of oxygen and SSDS. Propane is a gas used for barbecues, portable stoves, and as a vehicle fuel. Huffing propane can cause SSDS.

Propane and butane are flammable gases.

Communities Torn Apart

Inhalant and solvent abuse has been blamed for a number of deaths of young people on Native reserves in northern Canada. In some communities, children as young as six huff gasoline fumes from plastic bags and rags. The gasoline is siphoned from snowmobiles and other vehicles.

In 2004, the chief of the Sheshatshiu Innu community in Labrador went public with his community's ongoing struggle with solvent abuse. The Innu of Sheshatshiu were among the last aboriginal peoples to give up their nomadic way of life and settle in permanent communities in the 1960s. The dramatic transition led to the loss of traditional ways of life, crushing poverty, powerlessness, and alcohol abuse by older generations.

The children turned to gas sniffing as a way to numb their pain. The Sheshatshiu Innu did not have the resources to fight addiction, which requires treating both the physical and emotional needs of sniffers and keeping them away from the influence of other addicts.

Poppers

A fourth category of inhalants is nitrites. Both amyl nitrite and butyl nitrite are commonly known as poppers, but are sold as room deodorizer or VCR head cleaner. Unlike other solvents, the nitrites act differently on the nervous system. Poppers are frequently used to heighten sexual experiences because of they act as relaxants. Popper users are more at risk for unsafe sex and statistics show there is a higher rate of sexually transmitted diseases (STDs) and HIV/AIDS infections among users of these inhalants.

Quick High

Inhalants and solvents affect users differently, depending upon their age, prior use, and how much has been inhaled. The use of other drugs, and the user's sensitivity to the chemicals in the inhalant or solvent can also have an affect. All inhalants quickly enter the bloodstream through the lungs. Most users will experience a high within seconds to minutes. Highs can last anywhere from a couple of minutes to an hour. Many users will inhale a number of times in a row to make their high last a longer period of time.

Inhalants and solvents disrupt impulses to the brain. The younger the user, the higher the risk for brain damage and longer periods of use.

Altered States

Volatile solvents cause a high that is similar to being drunk on alcohol, but with greater **distortion** of **perception**, shapes, color, space, and time. The high is brief and often followed by drowsiness and either sleep or loss of consciousness. Some solvent users feel giddy, happy, and outgoing, while others experience fantasies, delusions, and hallucinations. It is also common to feel sick to your stomach or have headaches, slowed reflexes, and blurred vision either while using inhalants or immediately afterward. Nitrous oxide, or laughing gas, is ordinarily inhaled from a balloon and creates an intense, but short buzz or high. Nitrous users frequently have hallucinations, lose motor control, and experience an increased threshold for pain. Nitrous oxide is also known for producing a dream-like state of mind in which the user feels as though they are floating out of their body.

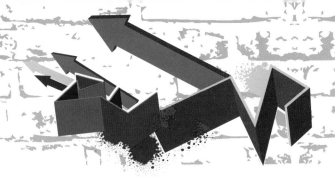

Chapter 3
Head Games

Inhalants and solvents are powerful psychoactive agents. The high they cause is short term, while the damage they do is long term. The dangers of inhalants and solvents are linked to how chemicals in the blood transfer to various body tissues. Solvents transfer easily into fatty tissue, so these chemicals build up quickly and continue to have effects long after the abuse has stopped.

Some of the short-term effects of sniffing or huffing are headaches, nausea, vomiting, and feeling lightheaded or dizzy. Inhalant users often feel disoriented for several hours or days after use. Reckless behavior is also a serious risk as users may be more likely to do things they might not normally do, such as having unprotected sex, jumping off of things, or driving while high.

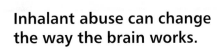

Inhalant abuse can change the way the brain works.

Suffocation

Users can die from suffocation because many inhalants are breathed into the body through a bag. Bagging severely cuts down on the amount of oxygen in the blood and amplifies the effects of solvent vapors. These two factors cause many users to lose consciousness while inhaling. While unconscious, users can suffocate because the bag is pressed firmly to the mouth and they cut off their air. Inhalants and solvents are also poisonous to our bodies, so when they are inhaled it is especially common for first-time users to vomit. Many inhalant users die from choking on their own vomit while unconscious.

Asphyxiation

Users can also asphyxiate on the vapors that they have inhaled. Some inhalants and solvents are heavier, or more dense, than oxygen. In these cases, users may lose consciousness and fail to breathe in the oxygen needed to survive. As the lungs have no oxygen for the body and the inhaled gases are heavier than oxygen, the user has to deliberately and forcefully exhale to remove them from their lungs. When unconscious, some users are unable to do this and die from lack of oxygen.

When Your Heart Stops

The heart is especially affected by inhalant and solvent use. Inhalants and solvents such as butane and some aerosols **sensitize** the heart to noradrenaline. Noradrenaline is a chemical released by the body that increases the user's heart rate when they experience stress. When the heart is flooded with noradrenaline, an irregular heartbeat develops and can cause the heart to stop beating completely. In these cases, users often die within minutes.

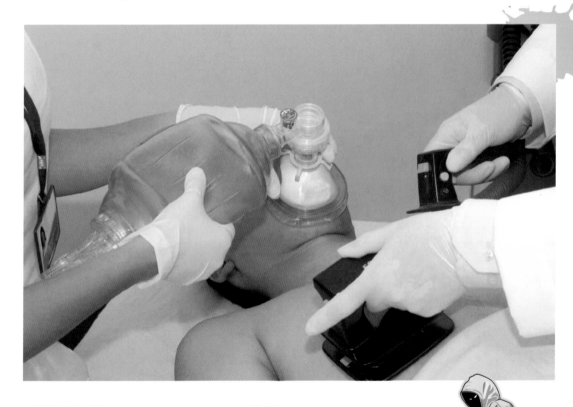

Whippets and Nangs

On the street, whippets or nangs are whipped cream chargers filled with the gas nitrous oxide that is used to whip cream in dispensers. They are also used as inhalants.

Reckless Behavior

Huffing makes you high and unable to think clearly. It is difficult for anyone to make smart decisions when they are not thinking straight. You could feel very powerful and strong. You could decide to have unprotected sex, not thinking about the consequences such as an unplanned pregnancy or sexually transmitted diseases. Huffers may also make other rash decisions, such as jumping off a bridge, believing they won't get hurt. Some users feel depressed as a result of inhaling and have suicidal thoughts.

Sores, Blisters, the Smell of Paint

It's often easy to identify long-time or "chronic" inhalant abusers. Huffers and sniffers develop sores around the mouth caused by irritation from the chemicals in solvents and inhalants. Users' clothing may begin to smell like chemicals. Users may also have

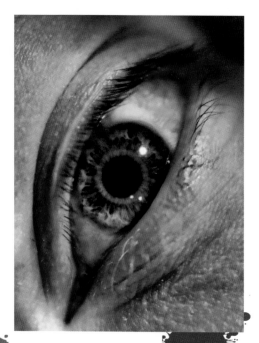

paint or other dyes on their hands, face, or clothing. Long-term users also become increasingly tired, thirsty, pale, and may have nosebleeds, bloodshot eyes, or they may be very thin from not eating when they are high. These outside symptoms are really only the tip of the iceberg. The serious damage done by inhalant and solvent abuse occurs inside the body over the long term.

In the Blood

Once inhaled, the chemicals in inhalants and solvents circulate rapidly through the user's bloodstream. They are deposited in all different types of tissues and affect many areas of the body. Inhalants and solvents gather in the myelin sheath, a protective fatty tissue that surrounds nerves, or neurons, in our brain and nervous systems. They break it down and make it more difficult for neurons to communicate effectively. Once this begins to happen, the impulses that travel through neurons can be misdirected or "jerky." Over time, permanent damage can be done to nerves because of breaks in the myelin sheath. Long-term users will have limb spasms and jerky movements.

Kids huffing openly on the streets of Nepal.

Long-Term Abuse

Long-term inhalant and solvent abuse can cause serious damage to major internal organs, such as the heart, lungs, kidneys, and liver. Users also risk bone marrow and brain damage. The chemical toluene, found in spray paint, has been linked to hearing loss and liver and kidney damage from long-term abuse. Hexane, a chemical in glue, can cause limb spasms and blackouts. Benzene, a common chemical in gasoline, has been shown to contribute significantly to bone marrow damage.

Huff Head

Through chronic abuse of inhalants, it is possible to do severe damage to the cerebellum. The cerebellum is the part of the brain that coordinates movement and muscle use. The cerebral cortex is also known to atrophy, or grow weak, through long-term huffing and sniffing. This part of the brain is involved in activities such as thinking, sensing, as well as in our use and understanding of language. Other **neurological** and psychological problems that can develop through chronic abuse include delusions, **dementia**, depression, or seizures.

Huffing messes with your ability to control your body's movements.

Street Lingo

On the street, slang terms like "hippy crack" or "Satan's secret" are used to refer to the danger of abusing these chemicals. Danger has credibility on the street and can entice others into trying something either as a dare or because of the risk. On the other hand, inhalants are also referred to as "moon gas" or "Oz." Through these names, users refer to the dreamy and distorted effects that inhalants can produce when abused. The other-worldly effects of inhalants are also used to lure users to enter the dream-like state of intoxication.

It's easy to become hooked on huffing and snorting, but the first high can never be duplicated and can cause irreversible health problems. It's just not worth the risk.

Chapter 4
Inhalant History

The inhaling of gases started in ancient times, and humans have used a number of substances to get high, or numb themselves from the pain of medical operations. In ancient Greece, the **oracle** at the Temple of Apollo in Delphi made predictions about the gods and the future while in a trance. According to legend, the oracle sat on a bench over a crack in Earth's surface from which flowed a sweet smelling-gas. The Greeks interpreted the oracle's trance as a connection to a god-like state of awareness. Modern scientists have since discovered the area around the oracle's temple released mind-altering gases that flowed through small cracks in the earth. The oracle wasn't seeing into the future—she was high on inhalants.

Gas escaping from the earth.

29

Into the Ether

Many early inhalants were pain relievers and anesthetics used to make people unconscious for surgery. Ether is a flammable chemical solvent that has been distilled for centuries—and it was a popular drug for a time in the 1800s. The famous painter and poet Dante Gabriel Rosetti died due to poor health related to an ether addiction. Ether was also used as an anesthetic in medical operations in the 1800s until it was replaced with modern anesthetics.

Laughing Gas

Nitrous oxide, or laughing gas, is a colorless and odorless gas used as an anesthetic in dentistry. Laughing gas got its reputation for giving users the giggles when it was used at laughing gas parties in the 1800s. It was first used as an anesthetic in 1844. It is still used today, although it is strictly regulated.

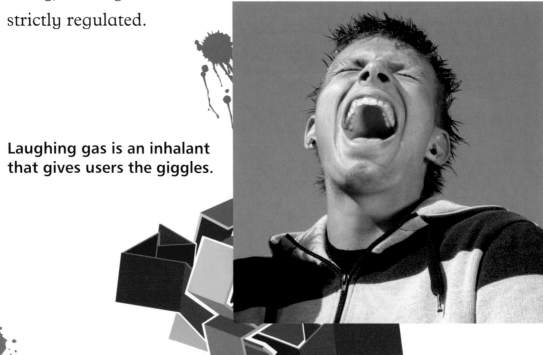

Laughing gas is an inhalant that gives users the giggles.

Inhaling Household Products

Inhalant and solvent abuse did not become a major problem until the 1950s, when volatile solvents became widely available in household cleaning products. Even when used as directed, many chemical cleaners give off fumes. It was not until a news story in 1959 publicized some isolated cases of glue sniffing that inhalant abuse took off. The story described both how to sniff glue and its intoxicating effects. Within weeks, there were examples of copycat sniffers. Shortly thereafter, the intoxicating effects of a large number of inhalants and solvents became known. Despite the use of educational programs and scare tactics, a culture of inhalant and solvent abuse had taken hold.

A "gluey" is a person who is known to sniff glue. "Glue shoe" refers to an intoxicated feeling that glue sniffers experience when their legs feel tired.

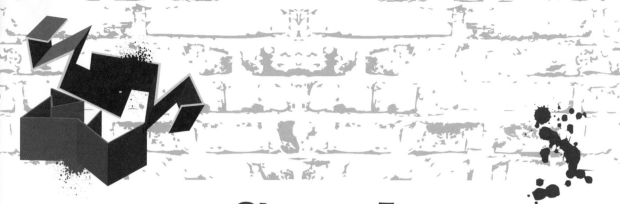

Chapter 5
Dependence and Addiction

Using inhalants and solvents does not solve problems. In fact, both the short-term and long-term health risks are so severe that using is never a good decision. If you are already using, or are considering doing so, educate yourself about the dangers of addiction. Statistics show that people who have all the facts about drug use and abuse are less likely to get involved with them.

Drug addiction and dependence are serious issues. Most users of inhalants and solvents do so only occasionally and experimentally and never develop an addiction. Inhalants and solvents are considered gateway drugs, so young people who experiment with them are more likely to use other street drugs in the future. Young people who use gateway drug often continue these patterns of behavior with street drugs. Gateway drug use is generally a reliable predictor of future drug use.

Dependence and Mood Disturbances

Addiction to inhalants and solvents occurs gradually. In the beginning, they are used recreationally, perhaps just on weekends or when others are doing them. Users enjoy the high or buzz created by the drugs and want to experience it more frequently. Soon, users are getting high every weekend and one or two nights a week. At this point, users often start to feel either physical or psychological cravings when they are not high.

Cravings are feelings that make getting high seem not only appealing, but necessary. Many addicts describe cravings as an itch that they have to scratch. Physical cravings are bodily sensations that result from withdrawal from a drug. When a drug is present in the body for a long period of time, cells become habituated, which means the cells are used to the drug's presence. When the level of this drug drops, the cells start to react to its absence. The body's cells create uncomfortable sensations when the drug is absent. These physical cravings make it hard to think about anything other than getting and using the drug.

Urges and Panic

The need to get high can feel like a life or death situation for an addict. Many addicts really think and feel they will die if they do not get high. Often this feeling is made worse when the addict becomes "drug sick" or feels ill because they have not gotten high.

Mental Addiction

When a user gets high all the time, the brain becomes used to the feeling of being high. When a user comes down, he or she may have psychological cravings or thoughts and impulses that drive the them to want to get high again immediately. They think about it all the time. The addict's physical and psychological cravings reinforce their desire to get high and make it even harder to break free.

Drug Tolerance

Habitual huffers develop a tolerance to the substances they inhale. Tolerance happens when the user's body is used to the presence of inhalants and solvents, and a higher dose is required to get high. Tolerance and cravings create a negative feedback loop. Users want to get high more often because of their cravings but, because of their tolerance, they need to use more frequently and in larger quantities to experience a high.

Drug tolerance can make what was once a cheap high very costly.

Withdrawal

When someone is addicted to an inhalant or solvent, their body becomes used to its presence. If the drug is no longer inhaled, the addict begins to experience withdrawal. As the drug's presence disappears, the addict's body will react. Withdrawal from inhalants and solvents can make a user physically sick with flu-like symptoms, tremors, severe anxiety, depression, loss of appetite, and **paranoia**. Even though these withdrawal symptoms are uncomfortable, a user can get through them. The health benefits of stopping use far outweigh any withdrawal symptoms.

The highest rates of inhalant and solvent addiction occur among homeless and street youth who live in poverty.

Behavior Changes

If you have a friend who huffs regularly, you may notice changes in their behavior that make them difficult to be around. Users will sometimes lie about what they are doing or where they are going. They may do anything to get their drug of choice, including stealing from people they love. Addicts often make up elaborate lies to justify why they are acting as they do. Lying is also used to avoid confrontation with friends, family members, or authority figures. Users often begin to cut off people in their life who do not know about their addiction. They may isolate themselves, and hang around and use with other inhalant and solvent addicts only. As the addiction becomes the central focus in their life, they may cut off contact with almost all others.

Addicts often defend their drug use, arguing that they are not addicted. Some are ashamed of their use and how they cannot control it, or stop using.

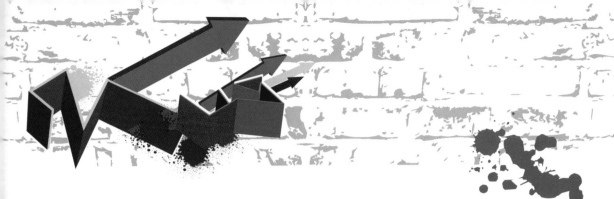

Chapter 6
Seeking Help

It takes guts to admit you have a problem—or to support a friend who needs help. You have to be honest, and this is often one of the most difficult things. Drug use often develops out of trying to avoid, deny, or escape the reality that surrounds us. So coming to terms with it is a big step in a positive direction.

Addicts will often say "I don't need to sniff, I do it because I like it," or "all my friends are huffing, so it has to be alright." Many think they don't have a problem and can stop using whenever they want. Some may just use on weekends and think that this means that they are in control. None of these statements are true. They just prevent addicts from seeing the extent of their abuse.

Crisis Management

Many users have to go through a crisis to stop. Some users develop health problems or have an accident before realizing what they are really doing. Others may even lose a friend to sudden sniffing death or suffocation before realizing they want to quit. A crisis does not need to happen, some addicts are just done with it.

The First Step

The first step in getting help is simply admitting that you have a problem with sniffing or huffing. Doing so may make you feel ashamed or guilty. These emotions are normal. Admitting you have a problem can feel like telling yourself a secret that you have been hiding. At some level, you knew you had a problem, but you were unable to be honest about it, even with yourself. This is what kept your desire to get high from disappearing.

Ask for Help

The next thing you need to know is that you cannot do this alone. Whether it is a trusted friend, family member, health professional, teacher, or counselor, you need to talk to someone about what is happening. This is called disclosure. Disclosing inhalant and solvent use does not feel easy, but you will likely feel an immediate sense of relief. You may feel better just because someone else knows. It is very important that you pick the right person to confide in. Avoid someone who judges you for your choices and behavior. Try to chose someone who can support you and help you get clean.

Reaching Out

It is hard to kick a habit that you may have enjoyed at one time. You may have started using to forget about problems or trauma. Stopping use will bring those problems back up. Psychologists and addiction counselors can help you get to the root of your addiction.

People Who Can Help

Inhalant and solvent abuse is serious and it is important that you feel safe disclosing. Trust and safety go hand-in-hand. If you do not feel safe talking to a parent, friend, or teacher, there are other options. Crisis lines can help you get in touch with people who can lend a hand and help you get treatment for your addiction. These lines are anonymous, so you don't have to identify yourself or be "outed."

The initial steps of disclosure can feel difficult. When you first reveal your inhalant abuse to another person, they may be initially shocked or surprised. Some will be relieved you came to them. Avoiding inhalants is key to breaking the habit. This will mean staying away from others who abuse inhalants and solvents. This will be difficult, because it means leaving friends behind.

Just knowing that somebody else shares your secret can make the situation easier to handle.

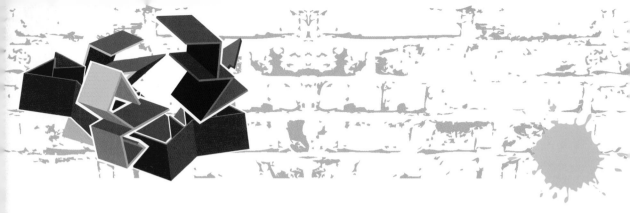

Chapter 7
Treatment and Recovery

Treatment and recovery are slow processes for sniffers and huffers. It can take several months for users to detoxify, since the chemicals in inhalants and solvents are stored in the body's fatty tissue. Treatment at a drug rehabilitation facility is ideal, but sadly it is not always available to everyone.

Length and Degree of Addiction

The length of time treatment takes varies based on a user's length and level of addiction, the age of the user, and the user's support network of friends and family. You may think that it is impossible for you to quit inhalants and solvents. Often, by the time people are ready for treatment, they are sick and tired of their addiction but also afraid to kick it. Treatment usually takes two forms: behavioral and pharmacological (using prescription drugs).

For inhalant abuse, behavioral therapy is the most common mode of treatment. The aim is for users to learn to recognize behaviors that trigger a desire to use inhalants.

Treatment Strategies

Drug treatment workers understand the physical and psychological sides of cravings and offer strategies to help users deal with them. These strategies are learned in a safe environment, whether alone or in a group, to help users gain strength for avoiding inhalant-abuse situations. Users will be encouraged to understand why they turned to inhalants and solvents. Ideally, drug rehab facilities are nonjudgmental environments for users to discuss addiction and strategies to avoid abuse.

Relapse Is Common

After a user has stopped abusing inhalants for a period of time, and their body detoxifies, they can begin the process of recovery. In many cases, recovery is a long process that has setbacks and requires hard work. Relapse is also very common. A relapse happens when a user who has successfully stopped abusing inhalants begins using them again. A relapse can be short (one instance of huffing or sniffing) or as long as several months or years of abuse. Addiction counselors aim to help addicts understand what relapse is and how to prevent it. For some people, the road to recovery has many relapses, while others may have none. The most important thing in dealing with drug addiction is getting on, or back on, the road to recovery.

Support Networks

Overcoming addiction is not something easily done on your own. Users need support networks of friends and family, as well as professional addiction counselors. There are a wide range of health networks and support groups that are available to support inhalant and solvent users. If you don't have a support network and don't know who to trust, phone a crisis line. Crisis line staff are knowledgeable and trained. They will try to connect you with resources for support.

Resources

Inhalants and solvents are powerful household chemicals that are often abused because they are cheap, legal, and easy to access. There is a lot of helpful information on inhalant and solvent abuse. Here are some trustworthy resources that can help you:

Books

Inhalants & Solvents: Sniffing Disaster by Noa Flynn (Mason Crest Publications, 2007). This is a useful guide to the harm done by inhalant and solvent abuse and why it is such a big problem.

Websites

TeensHealth: Inhalants
www.kidshealth.org/teen/drug_alcohol/drugs/inhalants.html
This informative website provides good resources and information about how inhalants and solvents affect health, signs of addictions, and getting treatment.

NIDA for Teens: Inhalants
www.teens.drugabuse.gov/facts/facts_inhale1.php
The National Institute on Drug Abuse's teen website on inhalants has excellent background information and statistics on inhalant use, short- and long-term health effects from use, and resources for seeking help and/or treatment.

SAMHSA: Substance Abuse Treatment Facility Locator
www.findtreatment.samhsa.gov/
This Substance Abuse and Mental Health Service Administration website rapidly connects substance abusers with treatment locations and options in their state and close to their home.

Office of National Drug Control Policy: Inhalants
www.whitehousedrugpolicy.gov/streetterms/ByType.asp?intTypeID
    =34
This is a government-maintained website that lists different street names for inhalants and solvents.

Organizations, Hotlines, and Helplines

National Suicide Prevention Lifeline (1-800-273-TALK)
(USA only)
This number can be used by individuals who need a confidential or anonymous place to talk about substance abuse and other issues.

Treatment Referral Helpline (1-800-662-HELP) (USA only)
The Substance Abuse and Mental Health Service Administration's helpline connects those in need with appropriate local networks and facilities to begin treatment and recovery.

Kids Help Phone (1-800-668-6868) (Canada only)
Provides bilingual, confidential, and anonymous support for kids in Canada encountering many different issues and problems.

National Youth Crisis Hotline (1-800-442-HOPE)
A general 24-hour, 7-day-a-week crisis line that can refer you to local drug treatment centers for counseling and help.

Glossary

accelerant A substance that speeds something up, or makes it go faster

aerosol A substance in a container under pressure and able to be released as a fine spray through the use of a gas

anesthetic A substance that makes a person insensitive to pain or unable to feel pain

asphyxiate To die after being deprived of air necessary to breathe

dementia A disease that causes memory lapses, personality changes, and an inability to think clearly

depressive Something that causes feelings of hopelessness and sadness

disorienting Something that makes someone confused

distortion Pulling or twisting out of shape, or making something different from how it really is

evaporate To turn from a liquid to a vapor

inhalants A gas or liquid breathed in or inhaled

intoxication To cause someone to lose control over their body or behavior

nervous system The system, which includes the brain, spinal cord, and nerves, that controls the actions and reactions of the body

neurological Belonging to the nerves or nervous system

oracle A priest or priestess who gave advice or made predictions called prophesies that were claimed to be from the gods

paranoia A mental condition characterized by delusions or extreme unwarranted fear

perception A person's ability to see, hear, or be aware of something through the senses

propellants A substance that causes something to move or be driven forward under pressure

sensitize To cause something to be sensitive or be easily affected by slight changes

siphoned To use a tube or pipe to draw off or transfer liquid from a container into another

solvents A liquid that forms a solution used for cleaning or industrial use

volatile A substance that changes rapidly or unpredictably from one thing to another

Index